FUNDAMENTALS

OF

PENTECOSTAL ONENESS

HARRY L. HERMAN, D.D., TH.D.

EDITOR-IN-CHIEF

Eric A. Beda, MBA

ALPHA OMEGA
PUBLISHING

Published in the United States by
Alpha Omega Publishing Company
P.O. Box 353, Jackson, MI 49204
Library of Congress Control Number: 2017962179

ISBN: 978-0-9985799-6-2

All Scripture quotations are derived from the Holy Bible, King James Version and the New King James Version.

Alpha Omega Publishing Company publishes books that promote the discussion and understanding of the Pentecostal movement throughout the world since the day of Pentecost. These books are made possible by the enthusiasm of our readers; the support of a committed group of donors, large and small; the collaboration of our many partners in the independent media and ecclesiastical organizations; booksellers, who often hand-sell Alpha Omega Publishing books; librarians; and above all by our authors. Books may be purchased in quantity and/or special sales by contacting the publisher:

Alpha Omega Publishing
517-879-1286
E: info@omegapublishing.org
www.omegapublishing.org

Printed in the United States of America

This book is dedicated to the men and women who are students of the Bible and for ministers to use as a tool to better understand the Pentecostal Oneness message.

Table of Contents

Acknowledgments

First of all, this work is dedicated to my Lord and Savior, Jesus Christ, whose spirit of inspiration and revelation is the source of the contents of these writings.

Further, I would like to dedicate this book to my wife, Dr. "Jerry" Herman for her generous expertise in editing my writings. She was never too busy to help in any way possible. It was her encouragement that prompted me to put on paper the basics of the teaching so dear to both of us.

This book is also dedicated to those learned and scholarly Bible teachers, who taught me so fervently in my formative years. Their lessons have not and will not be forgotten because they have instilled in me a knowledge and understanding of God through the inspired instruction of the Holy Ghost. Most have gone to be with the Lord, but the legacy of their ministry lives on to instruct and inspire a new generation of believers. It is my hope that this book, *Fundamentals of Pentecostal Oneness,* will be a channel through which the teachings of the "Fathers" may pass on to generations to come.

Preface

I thank thee, O Father, Lord of heaven and earth, because thou hast hid these things from the wise and prudent, and hast revealed them unto babes [born again Christians].

Matthews 11:25

This book is written for individuals who crave the pure spiritual milk of the Word of God, so that by it one may grow up in salvation and serve God wholeheartedly according to the right division of Scripture (1 Peter 2:2). This work is very precious to new ministers and new converts who will find this book as a valuable resource in understanding the basics of the Pentecostal Oneness message. The wise writer Solomon wrote, *"wisdom is the principal thing; therefore get wisdom: and with all of thy getting, get an understanding"* (Proverbs 4:7). A house without a stable foundation is destined to fall and be destroyed. These principles provide a foundation to begin building a new life in Christ and help develop an effective ministry pleasing and acceptable to God.

When you think of the *Fundamentals of Pentecostal Oneness*, think foundational, building blocks, knowledge, understanding, wisdom. Think of revelatory truth. Scripture says, "For precept must be upon precept, precept upon precept; line upon line, line upon line; here a little, and there a little" (Isaiah 28:10). The establishment of truth is as one that is building a structure. The structure begins with a cornerstone. Once the cornerstone is established then the foundation is built upon the surety of the cornerstone. When the foundation of the structure is laid then one can begin to build by laying bricks upon another until the structure is complete. This is how the church of God is built. Jesus Christ is the foundation and the chief cornerstone (Isaiah 28:16; Acts 4:10-12; 1 Peter 2:4-7).

The publication of this book underscores a genuine appetite for deep and revelatory knowledge about the right division of the Word of God concerning the revelation hidden in the gospel of Jesus Christ. With numerous voices around the prerequisites of New Testament salvation, it is needful to have a scriptural understanding of the subject.

These fundamentals offer believers a platform and a blueprint for the ministry of Christ. If these fundamentals be in you and abound, you will be neither barren nor unfruitful in the knowledge of our Lord Jesus Christ (2 Peter 1:8). It is my hope and prayer that this book equips and empowers you to develop a lifestyle that is inculcated in the work of the Pentecostal Oneness Fathers.

Éric A. Béda,

Editor-in-Chief

FUNDAMENTALS
OF
PENTECOSTAL ONENESS

Introduction

Whom shall he teach knowledge? and whom shall he make to understand doctrine? them that are weaned from the milk, and drawn from the breasts. For precept must be upon precept, precept upon precept; line upon line, line upon line; here a little, and there a little: for with stammering lips and another tongue will he speak to this people.

Isaiah 28:9-11

The substance of this book is especially important for newly converted Christians to become acquainted with the Oneness message. It is referred to by theologians as the Pentecostal Apostolic faith, the Apostolic faith, or simply the Apostolic Doctrine. The fundamentals of Oneness teachings are treated with considerable detail. Contained in this book are important subjects on the understanding of eternal security versus unconditional eternal security, and typical questions asked by those new to the Pentecostal Oneness faith.

Let us consider the questions in the Book of Isaiah chapter 28. Whom shall He (God) teach knowledge? Whom shall He make to understand doctrine (His teachings)? The Scripture addressed those questions, *"them that are weaned from the milk, and drawn from the breast."* What type of individuals are weaned from milk? First of all, what does milk illustrate? *"For when the time ye ought to be teachers, ye have need that one teach you again which be the first principles of the oracles of*

God; and are become such as have need of milk, and not of strong meat" (Hebrews 5:12; 1 Peter 2:2). Milk symbolizes the first principles or the fundamentals of the Word of God. Principle comes from a Latin word, principium, which means beginning; it includes the comprehensive and fundamental law, doctrine or assumptions.

The weaning process begins the first time a baby takes food from a source other than the breast of the mother – whether it's formula from a bottle or mashed food from a spoon. Weaning is the gradual replacement of breastfeeding with other foods and ways of nurturing. The human baby is considered weaned when the baby stops nursing and gets all its nutrition from sources other than the breast. Although babies are also weaned from bottles, the term usually refers to when a baby stops breastfeeding. Weaning doesn't necessarily signal the end of the intimate bond the mother and the child created through nursing. It just means you're nourishing and nurturing the baby in different ways.

Whom shall He (God) teach knowledge? He will teach those who are willing to hear and receive His Word. "He that hath an ear, let him hear what the Spirit saith unto the churches" (Revelation 2:29). There are those that are unwilling to hear His word. "*He that rejecteth me, and receiveth not my words, hath one that judgeth him: the word that I have spoken the same shall judge him in the last day"* (John 12:48). The words of Jesus Christ as He addressed the Israelites; those same words are echoing to us today, "*Why do ye not understand my speech? Even because ye cannot hear my word"* (John 8:43).

Whom shall He make to understand the doctrine? Doctrine is simply "the act of or result of teaching." He will teach and offer understanding to anyone who has a willing heart to hear Him. *"My son, give me thine heart, and let thine eyes observe my ways"* (Proverbs 23:26). God is pleading as He has always appealed to the heart of man, for an opportunity to see mankind turned toward Him. He is sensitive to us because He understands the very brittle nature of the human race. Hence, the Lord is patient toward man and He is slow to anger, and of great mercy, forgives our transgressions, and He is abundant in goodness and truth (Numbers 14:18).

And every one that heareth these sayings of mine, and doeth them not, shall be likened unto a foolish man, which built his house upon the sand: And the rain descended, and the floods came, and the winds blew, and beat upon that house; and it fell: and great was the fall of it. And it came to pass, when Jesus had ended these sayings, the people were astonished at his doctrine: For he taught them as one having authority, and not as the scribes (Matthew 7:26-29).

~1~
The Fundamentals

The *Fundamentals of Pentecostal Oneness* are foundational teachings taught by the Apostolic Fathers, including the apostles of Jesus Christ. The fundamentals are the starting point of a path that leads to perfection. These seven fundamentals embody the basic foundation of the Pentecostal Oneness message. These subjects will be addressed with a series of Bible verses relative to the following questions to offer a better understanding of the Oneness faith.

- What does repentance mean?
- How is baptism administered?
- What is the new birth?
- What is the Holy Spirit and how is it received?
- Who is Jesus Christ?
- What follows the new birth?
- What future can the new saint look forward to?

These seven subjects are the basics of what we are to believe and are important for any growth toward staying saved. As you review these fundamentals, the goal is to become full-grown, mature children of God with the ability to reflect the character of His righteousness and holiness in this world and preparing for the world to come.

These fundamentals are the essentials of the Pentecostal Oneness faith and cannot be expounded until they become the basic beliefs of the heart. Other aspects of the faith or goal of spiritual perfection hinge on believing these elements. Apostle Paul lets us know that the main objective is to know Christ and *"the power of his resurrection"* (Philippians 3:10). The goal of the ministry is to bring the people of God into the full knowledge of His will and to know the hope of His calling, the glory of His inheritance in the saints (Ephesians 1:18), and to acquire the knowledge of the son of God (Ephesians 4:11-16). Before this can happen, these fundamentals must be believed.

God's purpose before the foundation of the world was to have people that were *"holy, without blame before him in love"* and that these people would be granted eternal life (Ephesians 1:4; John 10:10). Before this could be a reality, the sin issue had to be resolved. Sin must be removed as a guilty stain from the person God wants to save. God, in the beginning, had a 'thought' of how to express himself on behalf of man. That 'thought' was God, who was made flesh and dwelled among us and was called the Son of God or Emmanuel-God with us. (John 1:1, 14; Matthew 1:23). That thought, in the mind of God, became a reality in the fullness of time (Galatians 4:4) and was the visible expression of the invisible God (Hebrews 1:1-3). A name was given to this Son. It was the name Jesus, the Savior of man (Matthew 1:21). It was He who came to be sin for us, to pay the price of our transgressions that we might be made the righteousness of God through Jesus (1 Corinthians 5:21; Isaiah 53). It was Jesus who first preached the gospel and delivered the procedure of salvation to His apostles. He commanded them to teach all nations that Jesus was the one and to also baptize in His **name** beginning at Jerusalem (Matthew 28:19; Luke 24:47; Hebrews 2:1-4). "Except we believe that He is the one, the only one, we cannot be saved and will die in our sins" (John 8:24; Acts 4:10-12).

Jesus Christ is the focal point of each of these fundamentals. When the gospel is preached and obeyed, repentance is the result as one turns from sin towards Christ. Jesus is the name and His shed blood is the means by which sins are remitted. The whole process began with our faith in the son of God, Jesus Christ. Jesus is the giver of the Holy Ghost, which is the Spirit of Christ sent down from Heaven as on the day of Pentecost. It is the same spirit received by believers when the apostles laid hands on them and it is the same spirit received by believers today.

Jesus will be sitting on His throne to judge all the souls of mankind ever born at the final judgment (Acts 17:31; John 5:22-30). If we believe these principles, then we must believe in Jesus as the Scripture declares Him to be (John 7:38).

Since these fundamentals are the basic teachings of Christ, who is the foundation Rock the church is built upon, it is absolutely essential that this foundation be firm and unchanged if it is to be victorious over the assaults of the gates of Hell (Matthew 7:24-27; 16:18). These fundamentals need no updating, revisions or additions, but must remain as they were first taught by Jesus Christ and the apostles, the fundamentals are the foundation on which the Pentecostal Oneness community stands on (Ephesians 2:20-22). This is the faith once delivered to the saints (Jude 1:3). A new generation of preachers may change them to suit their needs, but to do so would give the enemy, Satan, a sure victory.

~2~
Repentance

What does repentance mean? Is it necessary for salvation? Repentance is changing one's mind and attitude toward sin: wickedness, unrighteousness, and self-will. It is an act of turning towards God and His way. Moreover, it is the willingness to obey His word and serve Him. Repentance is to acknowledge from the heart 'I am wrong and God is right', then be willing to forsake your way to walk in God's way.

Steps to repentance: 1) hear the gospel, 2) believe and obey the gospel, 3) humble self, 4) cry out to God, and 5) turn from your way.

- Acts 17:25-31 God has commanded men everywhere to repent.
- Mark 1:15 Repent and believe the gospel.
- Luke 24:47 Repentance and remission of sin is to be preached in His name.
- Romans 2:4 The goodness of God leads to repentance.
- Isaiah 64:6 Our righteousness is as filthy rags in God's sight.
- Romans 3:23 All have sinned and come short of the glory of God.
- 2 Peter 3:9 God is not willing that any perish, but that all come to repentance.

- Job 33:14-20 God works to have men cease from their purpose and to seek His.
- Ezekiel 18:21-31 Let the wicked forsake his way.
- Job 40:4 Job saw himself as vile.
- Job 42:6 Job said, "*I abhor myself.*"
- Psalm 38:17 David said, "*I am ready to halt.*"
- Joel 2:12-13 Rend your hearts, not your garments.
- Psalm 34:18 A broken and contrite heart the Lord will not despise.
- Jonah 3:5-10 The people of Nineveh repented.

Evidence of Repentance

- Acts 26:16-20 Deeds worthy for repentance.
- Matthew 3:6-8 Bring forth fruit of repentance.
- 1 Thessalonians 1:9 They turned to God from idols.
- Isaiah 55:7 Let the wicked forsake his way.
- Jeremiah 31:18-19 They repented and were instructed and ashamed.
- Luke 15:17-21 The prodigal son came to his senses.

Repentance is a necessary aspect of God's plan for salvation. It is impossible for one to be the recipient of God's full salvation at the absence of a repentant heart.

~3~
Baptism

How is baptism administered? The term baptize is to immerse, to put under, buried, to make wet. Baptism is a washing and cleansing process (Acts 22:16; 1 John 1:7). The purpose of baptism is for the remission of sin (Acts 2:38).

- Romans 6:3-4 Buried with Him in baptism.
- Acts 2:38 Baptized in the **name** of Jesus Christ.

Atonement

Blood is the only substance God will accept for the expiation of the sins of men (Exodus 12:13; Leviticus 17:11; Hebrews 9:12-14, 22; Hebrews 10:4). In the Book of Matthew, the command is to baptize in the name of the Father, Son, Holy Ghost. The term **name** is singular and belongs to **one** person (28:19). Father, Son, and Holy Ghost are descriptive terms or offices of the one whose name is used. The name of the person represents that person -- to use his name is to exercise his authority. To baptize **in** equals baptizing into the **name**, thus becoming the 'property' of that one in whose name the baptism is performed (Galatians 3:27; Romans 6:3).

What is the name of the Father? What is the name of the Son? What is the name of the Holy Ghost? The name is **Jesus** (John 5:43; Luke 1:31; Matthew 1:21; John 14:26). This same Jesus is both **Lord** and **Christ** (Acts 2:36). The blood and name then become synonymous. It becomes impossible to get the benefit of the blood without using the **name** (Acts 4:17-18; Acts 5:23). Lord-Father (Spirit), Jesus-Son (flesh), Christ-anointing (Spirit).

Authority Is in the Name

- 1 Kings 21:8 The letters were written in the king's name (Esther 3:12).

- Acts 4:10-12 Jesus the only name for salvation.

- Luke 24:47 Remission of sin is preached in His name.

- Mark 16:17 In my name cast out devils.

- Colossians 3:17 Whatever you do, perform it in the name of Jesus.

- 1 Corinthians 6:11 Such were some of you, but now you are washed in the name of Jesus.

- Titus 3:5-6 The washing of regeneration is through Jesus Christ.

Jesus gave the command to be baptized as recorded in Matthew (28:19). He said to baptize in the **name** of the Father, and of the Son, and of the Holy Ghost. It is important to know what **name** to use. There's no conflict between the Book of Acts (2:38) and the Book of Matthew (28:19). The **name** as used in Matthew 28:19 is singular. All Peter did in Acts 2:38 was to provide the specific name-Jesus.

- Acts 2:38 Baptize everyone in the **name of Jesus**.

- Acts 8:12, 16 Samaria baptized in name of Jesus.

- Acts 10:36, 43, 48 Commanded to baptize in the **name of the Lord-Jesus**.

- Acts 19:5 The believers were baptized in the **name of the Lord-Jesus**.

- Acts 22:16 Paul was baptized calling on the **name of the Lord**.

- John 20:31 We have life through His **name**.

~4~
New Birth

What is the new birth? Jesus said, "You must be born again to see or enter the Kingdom of God" (John 3:3-5). Born again is to be born anew from above. The two elements of the new birth are **water and spirit** which together make the **one baptism.** Water -- baptism – spirit -- Holy Ghost. The new birth changes a sinful creature to a sinless one.

- Ephesians 2:1-5 We were dead in trespass and sin.

- Colossians 2:12-14 Buried with Him in baptism.

- Romans 6:1-4 Baptized to rise and to walk in newness of life.

- 2 Corinthians 5:17 If any be in Christ he is a new creature (creation).

- Galatians 3:27 Baptized into Christ is to put on Christ.

- Titus 3:5 The washing of regeneration - renewing of Holy Ghost.

The birth process is the result of two entities joining to form **one** new creature. As in a natural birth, there must be a conception before a birth can take place. One individual unilaterally cannot make a birth, there must be a male and a female involved in the begetting and conception process. In the spirit, there are two entities: the Word which impregnates the believer and **faith** to act on the Word received. The new birth presupposes the eradication of sin.

1. **Beget**. When a man fathers a child with a woman through the process of reproduction.

- 1 Corinthians 4:15 I (Paul) have begotten you through the gospel.

- James 1:18 Of His own will has He begotten us through the Word.

- Peter 1:23 We are born again of the Word of God.

- Romans 10:13-18 How can you hear without a preacher?

- 1 Peter 1:3 Begotten you unto a lively hope - resurrection of the dead.

- 1 Timothy 1:12 Death abolished and brought life and immortality to light through the gospel.

2. **Conception**. When the Word enters the heart of the individual.

- Romans 6:17 You have obeyed from the heart that form of doctrine (gospel).

- Ephesians 1:13 After you heard the word of truth you were sealed with the promise (the Holy Ghost).

- 1 Thessalonians 2:13 You received the Word not as from men, but as the Word of God.

- Acts 10:43-44 The Holy Ghost fell on them that heard the word of God.

- Luke 8:15 These are they who heard the Word (seed) and kept it.

3. **Birth**. The emergence of a baby or the beginning of life.

- Ephesians 1:13 You are sealed with the Holy Spirit of promise.

- Ezekiel 36:26 God to give a new heart and new spirit.

- Romans 6:1-4 We rise (from baptism) to walk in the newness of life.

- Isaiah 28:11 With stammering lips and another tongue God speaks to His people.

- Joel 2:28 I (God) will pour out my Spirit on all flesh.

- Acts 2:4 The day of Pentecost - they spake with other tongues as God gave utterance.

- Romans 6:13 Yield yourselves to God as those who are alive from the dead.

- John 5:24-26 We have passed from death unto life.

- Ephesians 2:1 He has quickened you who were dead in sin.

- Galatians 2:20 The life I now live, I live by the faith of Jesus Christ.

- 1 John 5:11-12 He that has the Son hath life.

- Colossians 1:13-14 We have been translated into the Kingdom of God's dear Son.

4. Family Relationship With God Through The New Birth

- Ephesians 2:18-19 We are fellow citizens of the household of God.

- 1 Corinthians 12:12-13 By one spirit are we all baptized into one body.

- 1 Corinthians 15:50 Flesh and blood does not inherit the Kingdom of God.

- Galatians 4:4-6; Romans 8:15-17; 1 John 3:2; Romans 8:9

~5~
The Holy Spirit

What Is the Holy Spirit and How Is It Received?

And when the day of Pentecost was fully come, they were with one accord and in one place. And suddenly there came a sound from Heaven as of a rushing mighty wind, and it filled all the house where they were sitting. And there appeared unto them cloven tongues like as of fire, and it sat upon each of them. And they were all filled with the Holy Ghost, and began to speak in other tongues as the spirit gave them utterance (Acts 2:1-4).

Then Peter said unto them, Repent, and be baptized everyone of you in the name of Jesus Christ for the remission of sins, and you shall receive the gift of the Holy Ghost (Acts 2:38). The Gospel of Luke shared, "*and, behold I send the promise of my Father upon you: but tarry ye in the city of Jerusalem, until ye be endued with power from on high*" (Luke 24:49). The Holy Ghost is the gift and promise made by God to give to His people.

- Luke 24:49 I will send the promise of my Father.
- Joel 2:28 A gift is something freely given for which no price is to be paid.
- Acts 1:4-8 Stay in Jerusalem until you receive the promise.
- Acts 2:3 Have received the promise of the Father.

- Ephesians 1:13 Sealed with the Holy Spirit of promise.
- John 20:22 Breathed on them and said, "receive ye the Holy Ghost".
- Joel 2:28 I will pour out my spirit on all flesh.
- Ezekiel 36:27 I will put my spirit within you.
- Zechariah 12:10 God to pour out His spirit of grace.
- Isaiah 44:3 I will pour out my spirit on your seed.
- Matthew 3:11 Jesus will baptize with the Holy Ghost and fire.
- Luke 11:13 Father to give the Holy Ghost to those who ask.
- John 4:10 If you had known the gift of God.
- John 4:14 The Holy Ghost is a well of water.
- John 7:37-39 Out of the belly shall flow rivers of living water.
- John 14:16-18 Give another comforter, the Spirit of truth.
- John 14:26 The Comforter which is the Holy Ghost.
- John 15:26 The Comforter whom I will send.
- John 16:7 It is expedient for you that I go away or the Comforter will not come.
- 2 Corinthians 1:21-22; 5:5 The anointing comes from God.
- 1 John 3:24; 4:13 We are His because of the spirit He has given.
- The Holy Ghost as the gift of God (John 4:10; Acts 2:38; 8:20; 10:45; 11:7; Hebrews 6:4).
- Romans 8:9 If ye have not the Spirit of God-Christ, then you are none of His.
- Acts 8:12-17 Apostles laid hands on them and they received the Holy Ghost. These had only been baptized but had not yet received the Holy Ghost.
- Acts 10:44-48 while Peter spoke, the Holy Ghost fell on them because they heard them speak with tongues.

- Acts 19:1-6 Receiving the Holy Ghost is the top priority.

The Holy Ghost Is God's Seal

- Ephesians 1:13 We are sealed with the Holy Spirit of promise.
- 2 Corinthians 1:21-22 God has sealed and given to us the earnest of His Spirit.

The Holy Spirit is the Spirit of Christ or the Spirit of God. Simply put, it is God residing in mankind.

~6~
Who Is Jesus Christ?

Who Is Jesus Christ? When Jesus came unto the coasts of Caesarea Philippi, He asked His disciples, saying, *"Whom do men say that I the son of man am?"* (Matthew 16:13).

- John 1:1, 14 In the beginning was the Word, and the Word was God... the Word was made flesh.

- John 4:24 God is a spirit and to be revealed He had to inhabit a body.

- John 1:18 No man has seen God at any time, the Son has revealed Him. Jesus, the son of God, is God revealed in a body of flesh for the purpose of redemption.

- John 1:29-30 Behold the Lamb of God which taketh away the sin of the world.

- Isaiah 43:6, 10-14 There is no God beside me, I am the First and Last.

- John 8:54-58 Before Abraham was I AM.

- 1 Timothy 3:16 God was manifest in the flesh.

- Hebrews 1:1-3 The Son is the express image of God.

- Colossians 1:15-17 Jesus the image of the invisible God.

- Colossians 1:19; 2:9 Fullness of the godhead dwells in him.

- 1 John 1:1 That which was in the beginning, we have seen, felt, and handled.

- Isaiah 9:6 The Son is the everlasting Father and the Mighty God.
- 1 John 5:20 Jesus is the one true God.
- Jesus is called Immanuel, God with us (Isaiah 7:14; Matthew 1:21-23).
- Jude 1:25 Jesus is the only wise God.
- 1 Timothy 1:17 The king eternal is invisible and He is the only wise God.
- 1 Timothy 6:15 The King of kings and Lord of lords.
- Revelation 17:14 He is Lord of lords, King of kings.
- Zechariah 14:9 The Lord shall be King.
- Jeremiah 10:10 The Lord is the true God and King.
- John 10:10 I and my Father are one.
- Acts 2:36 Jesus made both Lord and Christ.
- 1 Corinthians 12:3 We cannot call Him (Jesus) Lord but by the Holy Ghost.

JESUS CHRIST IS OUR SAVIOUR, REDEEMER, MEDIATOR

- Isaiah 48:11-12 I am He the first and the last. I do not give my glory to another.
- John 8:24 Except you believe that I am He, you will die in your sins.
- Isaiah 44:6-8 I am the First and Last, there is no God before me nor after me.
- Revelation 1:8, 11, 18 Jesus, He is the Alpha and Omega.
- Revelation 21:3-7 Our God is the Alpha and Omega.
- Matthew 28:18 All power in Heaven and earth is given to **Jesus**.

Jesus Christ is more than God's son. He is the Father, the Son, and the Holy Spirit. As Father, He is the creator of all things. All space is contained in Him. As Son, He is the redeemer and mediator between the fallen nature of mankind, and the merciful Almighty God. As Holy Spirit, He resides in the life of the believer.

~7~
After the New Birth?

AFTER THE NEW BIRTH, THEN WHAT?

Therefore we are buried with him by baptism into death: that like as Christ was raised from the dead by the glory of the Father, even so we also should walk in the newness of life.

Romans 6:4

Birth is the beginning of a living process that lasts a lifetime. Receiving the Holy Ghost, being born again, is not the finish line, but the start of a new lifestyle in Christ that involves experience, knowledge, and a spiritual education. When a baby is born, one of its basic instincts is the desire to be fed. By the same token, a healthy newborn saint has a desire to be fed, too. *"As newborn babes, desire the sincere milk of the word, that you may grow thereby"* (1 Peter 2:2). A baby knows nothing and must be instructed in things pertaining to life as it grows, and the same applies to the saints as they need to be 'educated' in the way of God for the acceptable conduct before man and God. Holiness is a new way of life, pleasing God and not ourselves (Hebrews 12:14).

We are to live a life that is patterned after the character and nature of Christ. As newborns, we are expected to grow in grace and knowledge of our Lord Jesus Christ.

- Galatians 2:20 The Life I now live I live by the faith of the Son of God.

- 2 Peter 3:18 Grow in grace and knowledge of Christ.

- 1 Peter 2:2 As newborn babes desire the sincere milk of the Word.

- Acts 2:42 They continued steadfast in the apostles' doctrine.

- John 8:31 If ye continue in my word, then you are my disciples indeed.

- Hebrews 6:1 Let us go on to perfection.

AS GOD'S CHILDREN, WE ARE EXPECTED TO PRODUCE FRUIT

- John 15:2-5 Every branch in Him ought to bring forth fruit.

- Galatians 5:22-25 The fruit of the Spirit.

- Romans 6:19-22 Yield your members unto righteousness and unto holiness.

- Ephesians 2:10 We are His workmanship to bring forth good works.

- Ephesians 4:13 We are to perfect the skills of Christ's nature until we come into His image, until we come into the fullness of Christ.

WE ARE INSTRUCTED ON HOW TO WALK WITH CHRIST

- Ephesians 4:1 Walk worthy of the vocation in which we have been called.

- Colossians 1: 10 Walk worthy of the Lord and fully pleasing Him.

- Hebrews 12:14 Holiness without which no man can see the Lord.

- Colossians 2:6-8 As you have received Christ, so walk in Him.

- 1 Thessalonians 2:12-13 The received word works effectively in us.

- 2 Corinthians 7:1 Cleanse yourselves from all filthiness of the flesh.

- Hebrews 12:1 Lay aside every weight and the sin that so easily besets us.

- Ephesians 4:22-32 Put off former manner of living and be renewed in our mind. We are to glorify God in our bodies and learn to please Him.

- 2 Corinthians 6:14 Come out from among them and be separated...holy unto God.

- 1 Peter 2:12; 3:15 Sanctify God before others.

- Romans 12:1-2 Present your bodies a living sacrifice holy unto God.

- Philippians 1:10 Approve things that are excellent.

Erik Erikson (1998) proposed a comprehensive psychoanalytic theory of psychosocial development encompassing eight stages in which a healthy developing individual from infancy to adulthood will experience. All stages are present at birth but only begin to unfold according to both a natural scheme and one's ecological and cultural upbringing. Unlike the finding of psychologist Erikson, God has a different development system for born-again Christians. The stages of spiritual development are not commonly discussed among Christians, but there are scriptural references and patterns about the level of those development. After born-again healthy developing Christians progress from the essentials of the Word then they move towards discipleship (Matthew 8:18-25; John 8:31). Afterward, the individual develops into the role of a servant (1 King 18:36; 2 King 5:20; 8:4; Numbers 11:28). The final stage is when Scripture references one as a friend of God (2 Chronicles 20:7; James 2:23). These spiritual developmental stages are not to be compared to secular development rather they are associated with one's involvement and commitment to ministry.

~8~
Future of Saints

What do the saints have to look forward to in the future? *"If in this life only we have hope in Christ, we are of all men most miserable"* (1 Corinthians 15:19). Jesus has promised us a better life now, but our real hope is in the life to come. It is the eternal life we long and wait for.

- Romans 8:18-22 The suffering of this life is not worthy to be compared to the glory that shall be revealed in us.

- 1 Timothy 4:8 Godliness is profitable in this life and in the life to come.

- 1 Peter 1: 3-4 We have a lively hope and an inheritance incorruptible reserved for us.

- Mark 10:28-30 We shall receive one hundred fold more in this life.

- Proverbs 29:18 Without a vision the people perish.

- 1 Thessalonians 1:10; 5:9 Delivered from the wrath to come.

- Isaiah 26:20 Come my people, enter into thy chambers.

- Jeremiah 10:10; Zephaniah l:15-17

- 2 Corinthians 4:16-18 Light affliction is but for a moment.

- 2 Corinthians 5:1-4 We have a house not made with hands.

- 1 Corinthians 15:42-58 We shall be changed.

- Philippians 3:20-21 He shall change our body and fashion it according to His glorious body.

- Revelation 1:6 He has made us kings and priests unto God and we shall rule and reign with Him.

- Revelation 20:6 Blessed and holy are those who are in the first resurrection.

- Titus 1:2 In hope of eternal life that God has promised.

- 1 John 3:2-3 We shall be like Him for we shall see Him as He is.

- 1 Thessalonians 4:14-18 The assurance of the rapture or resurrection for the church body.

~9~
How Many Ways to Salvation?

There is one Lord, one faith, and one baptism (Ephesians 4:5). There is only one way to salvation. For one to attempt to find another avenue is against the premise of the scriptures.

- John 10:1 To climb up any other way is thievery and robbery.

- Acts 4:10-12 By no other name but Jesus can one be saved.

- John 3:3-5 Except you are born again, you cannot see nor enter the Kingdom of God.

- Romans 8:9 If you do not have the Spirit of Christ, you are **none of His**. Is there another way? **No**!

Except one is born again by baptism in water in the name of Jesus and filled with the Holy Ghost as exhibited on the day of Pentecost one is not counted as one of God's children.

> *Not everyone that saith unto me, Lord, Lord, shall enter into the kingdom of heaven; but he that doeth the will of my Father which is in heaven. Many will say to me in that day, Lord, Lord, have we not prophesied in thy name? and in thy name have cast out devils? and in thy name done many wonderful works? And then will I profess unto them, I never knew you: depart from me, ye that work iniquity* (Matthew 7:21-23).

~10~
Oneness of the Godhead

It is not my purpose or intention to enter into a long detailed discourse about proving or justifying the Pentecostal Oneness tenet but to provide a short outline to acquaint my readers with this wonderful revelation of Jesus. The biblical references provided in our canonical is so extensive that time and space will not allow more than a brief glimpse into the wonders of our Lord and Savior, Jesus the Christ. Perhaps one of the most important planks in the Pentecostal Apostolic belief is the teaching of the **oneness** of God also known as the Jesus only message. The doctrine identifies those that believe this message as Apostolic.

The strict and absolute unity of God is the first principle of the Bible. The entire scope and spirit of both the Old and New Testaments are distinctly on the side of the unipersonality of God. The Jews who made Monotheism their boast and glory never charged Christ or the first teachers of Christianity with originating any new theory of the Godhead. Christ and the apostles spoke of the Father as the only true God. It is repeatedly admitted by Trinitarians that the word "Trinity" is not in the Bible; and that in the earliest records of Christian writings, not only is the word Trinity not found, but no equivalent of the word nor any proposition that characterizes God as three persons. Over the years, there have been countless authors that testified of the oneness of God.

The prophet Moses scribed, *"Hear, O Israel: The Lord our God is one"* (Deuteronomy 6:4). Jesus entertained questions from the scholars of His days on earth, including the Pharisees, the Herodians, and Sadducees when He was asked, *"Which is the first commandment of all? And Jesus answered him, The first of all the commandments is, Hear, O Israel; The Lord our God is one Lord" (Mark 12:29).*

Apostle Paul testified to the Corinthian church and shows the vanity of idols. As for eating of things that have been sacrificed to idols, an idol can do nothing in the world. However, to the saints, there is but one God, says the apostle, the Father of whom are all things and we are created for Him. We Christians are better informed because we well know there is but one God, the fountain of all beings, the author of all things, maker, preserver, and governor of the whole world, and of whom and for whom are all things exist. There is not one God to govern one part of mankind, and another to govern other aspects of creation. One God that made all things and has power over all. *"But to us there is but one God, the Father, of whom are all things, and we in him; and one Lord Jesus Christ, by whom are all things, and we by him"* (1 Corinthians 8:6).

Paul stated, *"there is none other God but one. One God and Father of all, who is above all." "One God and Father of all, who is above all, and through all, and in you all." "One God and one mediator between God and men, the man Christ Jesus"* (1 Corinthians 4:8; Ephesians 4:6; 1 Timothy 2:5).

It is not needful for the Holy Bible to seek nor require the affirmation of other sources, but it's respectable to know other notable personalities are aligned with it. The famous Mathematician and Scientist, Sir Isaac Newton supported monotheism as recorded in his writing,

There is One God, the Father, ever loving, omnipresent, omniscient, almighty, the Maker of Heaven and earth; and one Mediator between God and men-the man Christ Jesus. The Father is the invisible God. Christ came not to diminish the worship of the Father. It is not necessary to direct our prayers to any other than the Father in the name of the Son (Stannus, 1883).

William Penn founder of the Province of Pennsylvania supported the oneness of God in his body of work,

Before I shall conclude this head, it is requisite I should inform thee, reader, concerning the origin of the Trinitarian doctrine: Thou mayest assure thyself, it is not from the Scripture nor reason, since so expressly repugnant; although all broachers of their own inventions strongly endeavour to reconcile them with that holy record. Know then, my friend, it was born three hundred years after the ancient Gospel was declared; it was conceived in ignorance, brought forth and maintained by cruelty; for though he that was strongest imposed his opinion, persecuting the contrary, yet the scale turning on the Trinitarian side, it has, therefore, continued through all the Romish generations (Stannus, 1883).

There are many Christian denominations and individuals that identify as Pentecostals believe in the idea of speaking in other tongues and live a life of separation from the world yet they do not believe Jesus is God, the only true God (1 John 5:20). I am Pentecostal in experience and Apostolic in doctrine. Pentecostalism is an experience rooted in the conviction that speaking in other tongues is necessary as the initial evidence of one receiving the gift of the Holy Spirit. Oneness Pentecostals hold to the doctrine of the apostles of the New Testament, Jesus Christ, the true God. Herein lies the distinction between Pentecostal Oneness believers and other Christians, including non-oneness Pentecostals. The creed known as the Trinity was not taught by the apostles because all they learned and experienced was Jesus, the invisible God made visible and revealed in a body of flesh called the Son of God. In all references relative to God, there is no hint of a plurality of gods. Paul declared,

There is one body, and one spirit, even as ye are called in one hope of your calling; one Lord, one faith, one baptism, one God and father of all, who is above all, and through you all and in you all (Ephesians 4:4-6).

Israel's first instruction concerning God was, *"Hear O Israel: the Lord our God is one Lord: and thou shalt love the Lord thy God with all thine heart, and with all thy soul, and with all thy might"* (Deuteronomy 6:4-5). This statement establishes the fact that there is only one God. In response to the question, what is the first commandment? Jesus answered, *"The first of all the commandments is, Hear, O Israel; the Lord our God is one Lord"* thus confirming the existence of only one God (Mark 12:29). Heaven does not recognize more than one God and neither does Satan. *"Thou believest that there is one God; thou doest well: the devils also believe, and tremble"* (James 2:19). Since the Old and New Testaments confirm there is one God, then who is this one God and what is His name?

When Abraham had his encounter with the Almighty, God identified Himself as *"I am the Almighty"* (Genesis 17:1), the all sufficient God. The experience of Moses at the burning bush, God said, *"I AM that I AM, tell them that I AM sent you"* (Exodus 3:14). When Manoah spoke with the angel of the Lord, he asked: "What is thy name?" and the angel responded: *"Why do you ask, seeing it is secret?"* (Judges 13:18). The etymology of the word secret means 'wonderful', others say it is a mystery. To us in the Oneness faith, the name of God is truly wonderful, but no secret - it is Jesus, and only Jesus. Isaiah describes Israel's future Redeemer or King as: *"Unto us a child is born, unto us a son is given: and the government shall be upon his shoulder: and his name shall be called Wonderful, Counselor, The mighty God, The everlasting Father, the Prince of Peace"* (Isaiah 9:6). At the birth of Jesus, the angel announced His name was to be called Jesus - "For He shall save His people from their sins" (Matthew 1:21).

This one God has a variety of names and titles which were used to identify unique attributes of Israel's God. The name Jehovah was revealed as the covenant keeping God, the one who will establish a contract with His people and keep it. A portion of these titles were referenced as 'The Jehovistic Titles'. According to the *Hebrew Lexicon*, the Greek term, Jehovah, means Lord, "the existing One" (Genesis 4:1; Genesis 9:26;

Genesis 12:6). In the Old Testament, the most sacred name for God is Jehovah. Since it is sacred, it is never used to refer to any pagan gods neither is it used in regard to any human. It is reserved solely for the one true God alone. The name appeared nearly 6,823 times in the Old Testament, as He is the focus and hero of the Scripture.

Jehovah-Jareh (Genesis 22) means the Lord will provide. The name appeared as part of the story of Abraham in his ability to trust God due to his willingness to sacrifice his beloved son unto God. God commanded Abraham to sacrifice his son, Isaac. Abraham was fully persuaded to sacrifice his son to God because of his faith in God. However, when it was time to offer Isaac to the Lord, God provided a ram in the thicket.

And Abraham lifted up his eyes, and looked, and behold behind him a ram caught in a thicket by his horns: and Abraham went and took the ram, and offered him up for a burnt offering in the stead of his son. And Abraham called the name of that place Jehovahjireh: as it is said to this day, In the mount of the LORD it shall be seen (Genesis 2:13-14).

Abraham names the place of provision Jehovah-Jireh, which means "The LORD WILL PROVIDE". The sixth chapter of the Book of Matthew explains another great example of the Lord's faithfulness to provide. The disciples were concerned about their futures, what they and their families would eat, drink, and wear? Christ encouraged them to stop worrying because God knew that they had need of these things. He comforted them with words on how God provides for the birds and the lilies of the field. Look at the birds of the air; they do not sow, reap, or store away in barns and yet your heavenly Father feeds them. Are you not much more valuable than they? (Matthew 6:26, 30). If God clothes the grass of the field, which is here today and tomorrow is thrown into the fire, will He not much more clothe you, O you of little faith? Those who are in covenant relationship with God shall lack no provisions because He will provide.

Jehovah-Shamma means the Lord is there. It is the name given to New Jerusalem, a future city that was prophesied by Ezekiel through a vision. The name Jehovah-Shamma speaks of God's special presence with the people of God. Scripture says, "All the way around shall be eighteen thousand cubits; and the name of the city from that day shall be: THE LORD IS THERE" (Ezekiel 48:35). The Israelites were discouraged because they had been exiled by Babylon and their cities and temple had been destroyed. However, God gave Ezekiel a vision about a future city that would be far better than any previous cities. The vision was extremely encouraging to Ezekiel and the Israelites because earlier in Ezekiel's prophecies, God's presence had left the temple and the city of Israel altogether (chapters 8-11). It seems that there will be a future glorious city and a temple in Israel that are marked by the presence of God perpetually. God being there and present with His people is a reality today. The Book of Matthew reminds us of God's indwelling presence in every believer (Matthew 28:20). The Apostle Paul's words remind the saints,

Know ye not that ye are the temple of God, and that the Spirit of God dwelleth in you? If any man defile the temple of God, him shall God destroy; for the temple of God is holy, which temple ye are (1 Corinthians 3:16-17).

The saints are the temple of the living God because the Spirit of Christ which is the Holy Spirit is in them (1 Corinthians 6:19-20). He is in them and He is with them (the church) and that's what makes the gathering of the saints a special occasion. The gathering of the saints is about God's presence.

Jehovah-Tsidkenu, the Lord our righteousness (Jeremiah 23:5-6). Jehovah-Tsidkenu was the name given by God in the Book of Jeremiah for the Messiah. It means "The Lord Our Righteousness." The character of the Messiah that Israel was awaiting was righteousness. He would gather Israel from all the lands of the earth and He would rule over them. He would be a righteous shepherd and they would call Him "THE LORD OUR RIGHTEOUSNESS."

The days are coming, declares the LORD,

When I will raise up to David a righteous Branch, a King who will reign wisely and do what is just and right in the land. In his days Judah will be saved and Israel will live in safety. This is the name by which he will be called: The LORD Our Righteousness (Jeremiah 23:5-6).

Jesus, the Messiah, is the righteousness of the nation of Israel. He is the one that will eventually turn them from their sins and give them a new heart to follow Him (Romans 11:26). This is what Christ has already done for the saints. Christ took our sins while on the cross and gave us His righteousness. 2 Corinthians 5:21 says, "God made him who had no sin to be sin for us, so that in him we might become the righteousness of God."

Jehovah-Nissi (Exodus 17:15), the Lord our banner. The name is given in the context of warfare. When the Amalekites and Israel were at war and as long as Moses had his hands raised, Israel was victorious. Moses's hands being raised seemed to represent his prayers; therefore, dependence upon the God of Israel. Normally, when armies went to battle, the flag bearer would lead the way, representing the power and spirit of the nation. Similarly, when Israel went to battle, God went before them and led the way as their banner. As it was true for Israel, it is true for Christians today. God goes before His people. He makes our paths straight and He fights our battles. The Apostle Paul says to the church in Ephesus,

Finally, my brethren, be strong in the Lord, and in the power of his might. Put on the whole armour of God, that ye may be able to stand against the wiles of the devil (Ephesians 6:10-11).

Jehovah-Roi means the Lord is my Shepherd (Psalm 23). Jehovah-Roi is the name that David used concerning God in Psalm 23. He says, "The Lord is my Shepherd; I shall not be in want [lack or be without]" (Psalm 23:1). David serving as a shepherd in a certain season of his life understood the role of a shepherd in the life of the sheep. David referring to God as his shepherd, he understood the caring and protective role of the shepherd in the life of the sheep. As sheep, we are prone to stray and are vulnerable. Hence, we need a shepherd that leads, provides, and protects us; a shepherd that gives us rest and makes sure that we lack nothing. God is that shepherd. During David's time, shepherds were exposed to extreme temperatures, wild animals such as lions and wolves, and thieves. A shepherd that did not care for the sheep would simply run away when attacked. "A hireling, he who is not the shepherd, one who does not own the sheep, sees the wolf coming and leaves the sheep and flees; and the wolf catches the sheep and scatters them" (John 10:12).

Good shepherds are willing to give their lives for the sheep. Christ said, *"I am the good shepherd. The good shepherd lays down his life for the sheep"* (John 10:11). In fact, what makes our shepherd so amazing is that He even died for us. Our Lord Jesus Christ is not just a shepherd. He is the good shepherd. He provides for us, cares for us, and even gave His life for us. He is our Jehovah-Roi.

Jehovah-Shalom represents the Lord our peace (Judges 6:22-24). It is the name that Gideon ascribed to the Lord. Gideon saw the angel of the Lord and cries out about his demise because he saw a theophany of God. Scripture says to see God face to face meant death (Exodus 33:20); therefore, Gideon was afraid. However, the angel of the Lord comforted and reassured him, "Peace be unto thee; fear not: thou shalt not die" (Judges 6:23). Gideon built an altar unto the Lord there and called it, "THE LORD IS PEACE".

Scripture says, *"therefore, having been justified by faith, we have peace with God through our Lord Jesus Christ"* (Romans 5:1; 2 Corinthians 5:18). Christ has reconciled us to God by bringing peace in our relationship with God where before there was only hostility (Romans 5:10). Further, Paul urged the Philippian Christians by saying, *"Be anxious for nothing, but in everything by prayer and supplication, with thanksgiving, let your requests be made known to God; and the peace of God, which surpasses all understanding, will guard your hearts and minds through Christ Jesus"* (Philippians 4:6-7). Now, we do not only have *"peace with God"*, we also are given the "peace of God".

Jesus Christ says to His disciples, *"Peace I leave with you, my peace I give unto you: not as the world giveth, give I unto you. Let not your heart be troubled, neither let it be afraid"* (John 14:27). We will encounter troubles and difficulties in our lives, but in the midst of them, Christ wants us to have His supernatural peace. Therefore, we must let His peace rule in our hearts as we enjoy intimacy with Christ. Paul states in the Book of Colossians, "And let the peace of God rule in your hearts, to which also you were called in one body; and be thankful (3:15).

Jehovah-Roepha (Exodus 15:23-26) is interpreted the Lord our healer. The name that was used by Israel while they were in the wilderness. While journeying, they encountered bitter water at a place called Marah. God instructed Moses to throw wood into the water and as the wood made contact with the water, it healed the water and made it drinkable. Afterward, God instructed Israel saying if they obeyed His commands, He would be their healer. God's character to heal was manifested in the person of Jesus. When Christ came to the earth He healed the sick, the blind, the lame, and more than that He healed the hearts of people (Matthew 11:2-5). People who were separated from God and under His wrath, Christ reconciled them through His death (Isaiah 53:1-5; 2 Corinthians 5:18). He healed the terminal sickness of our souls and drew us back to God. The Apostle James testified and wrote,

> *Is any sick among you? let him call for the elders of the church; and let them pray over him, anointing him with oil in the name of the Lord: And the prayer of faith shall save the sick, and the Lord shall raise him up; and if he have committed sins, they shall be forgiven him (James 5:14-15).*

Jehovah-Sabaoth is interpreted the Lord of hosts or the Lord Almighty. The name portrays God as the ruler of the angels, the armies of Heaven. We see this image throughout the Scripture. The Sons of Korah said, *"The LORD of hosts is with us; the God of Jacob is our refuge"* (Psalm 46:7). The phrase

"LORD OF HOSTS" depicts God as a warrior and one who fights for the saints and protects us. Here is an illustration, Elisha is protected by an army of angels that surrounded his house (2 Kings 6:16-17).

These are a few of the Jehovah titles that Israel used to call on God for their unique needs. The advantage the saints have today is the simplicity of using the name **Jesus** for all our needs and worship. The first commandment on the tables of stone was, *"Thou shalt have no other gods before me"* (Exodus 19:20).

This one God is manifested in a threefold manner. First as **creator** (Father), **redeemer** (Son), and **anointing** (Holy Ghost). This does not make three gods in one package, but one God manifesting Himself in three different offices to fulfill the needs of a particular time. The clincher of Peter's dynamic sermon on the day of Pentecost was, "God hath made that same Jesus, whom ye crucified, both Lord and Christ" (Acts 2:36). As Lord, He is the Father, the creator of all things; as Jesus the Son, He is the Redeemer who delivers from sin; as Christ, He is the anointer and anointing-the Holy Ghost. Paul informs us clearly that all the fullness of God is poured into one package, the body of Jesus Christ, the Son of God. *"For it pleased the Father that in him [Jesus] should all fullness dwell"* and *"For in him dwelleth all the fullness of the Godhead bodily"* (Colossians 1:19; 2:9).

The Apostle John saw Jesus in His most lofty position and began his gospel with: *"In the beginning was the Word [Logos, the thoughts of God], and the Word was with God, and the Word was God,"* and subsequently, he said, *"And the Word was made flesh and dwelled among us"* (John 1:1, 14). God, before the foundation of the world, determined in His thoughts the form He would assume in His plan for salvation. He would use the image in His mind as a pattern by which Adam would be formed. In the fullness of time, God would overshadow a young maid with 'instructions' to build His earthly temple according to the thoughts already formed in His mind. By this process, God becomes the Father because Mary procreated a temple for Him to dwell in called the Son of God. God who is Spirit, confined Himself in that temple while at the same time serving as the God of the universe that fills all space. To some such concept seems mystical but others believe with God all things are possible. See Hebrews 10:5.

Philip asked Jesus to reveal the Father to the team of disciples and it will satisfy the state of obscurity about the Father. Jesus responded by saying,

> *Have I been so long time with you, and yet hast thou not known me, Philip? He that has seen me has seen the Father; -- Believest thou not that I am in the Father, and the father in me? The words that I speak unto you I speak not of myself; but the father that dwelleth in me, he doeth the works (John 14:7-11).*

Later, John began his first epistle with, *"That which was from the beginning, which we have heard, which we have seen with our eyes, which we have looked upon, and our hands have handled, of the Word of life"* (1 John 1:1). The one that John saw, handled, and listened to, is the same God who was in the beginning and was made flesh. It was so important for Jesus to be identified with the Father that He declared, *"I and my father are one"* (John 10:30). When the unbelieving Jews asked Jesus, *"Where is thy Father?"* then He answered, *"If ye had known me, ye should have known my Father also" (John 8:19).* He continued this dialogue by saying,

> *Ye are from beneath; I am from above: ye are of this world; I am not of this world [that is from heaven]. I said therefore unto you, that ye shall die in your sins: for if ye believe not that I am he, ye shall die in your sins (vs 23-24).*

The conversation revolved around Jesus and His Father. He simply stated that if you do not associate me and my father as one and the same, you will die in your sins without hope. Later in verse 27, they understood that Jesus spoke of Himself as the Father. Since redemption requires a blood sacrifice, it was necessary for God to take on a physical form in order to become the redeeming sacrifice man needed. God in the beginning and in His original existence is spirit. Since a spirit has no blood His intention was to provide a body for Himself, which would have the same nature as the creatures being redeemed. This body would provide the necessary blood sacrifice for the redemption of humanity; the invisible spirit embodying visibility and substance through the Son of God without ever ceasing to be the Almighty God.

> *Forasmuch then as the children are partakers of flesh and blood, he [God - Spirit] also himself likewise took part of the same; that through death he might destroy him that had the power of death, that is, the devil - For verily he [God] took not on him the nature of angels; but took on him the seed of Abraham (Hebrews 2:14,16).*

> *God, who at sundry times and in divers manners spake in time past unto the fathers by the prophets, hath in these last days spoken unto us by [through] his Son, whom he has appointed heir of all things, by whom also he made the worlds; who being in the brightness of his glory, and **the express image of his person**, and upholding all things by the word of his power, when he by himself purged our sins, sat down on the right hand of the majesty on high (Hebrews 1:1-3).*

Several things are to be noted in these verses. First, God speaks to the dispensation of our time through the agency of His sonship, Jesus Christ. Second, this Son is the owner of all things. Third, through the office of the sonship the worlds were created. Jesus is the **express visibility** of the invisible God. The only way God can be seen is through His manifested form called Jesus, the Son of God. Lastly, to sit on the right hand of the majesty on high is not a position, but in the favor God invested in the sonship. As Jesus prepared to depart from earth, He declared that *"all power is given unto me in heaven and in earth"* (Matthew 28:18). All things are subject to Him and He is in control. God will not give His glory to another (Isaiah 48:11) but has so determined that *"at the name of Jesus every knee should bow, of things in heaven, and things in earth, and things under the earth; and that every tongue should confess* *that Jesus Christ is Lord to the glory of God the father"* (Philippians 2:10-11; Romans 14:11; Isaiah 45:23). In addition, the Book of John (5:23) states, *"We are to honor the Son even in the same manner as the Father."* If we are to give proper honor to God then it must be done through Jesus Christ.

The following scriptural references will provide a base for research and study which will open a door to a better understanding of who Jesus is and the Oneness message.

OUR GOD WILL COME

- Isaiah 40:3-11 A voice in the wilderness crying, prepare the way of the Lord-- make a highway for **our God.** Who was their God? Jesus.
- John 1:23 John the Baptist was that voice announcing Jesus, Israel's God.
- Micah 5:2 The one to come whose going forth have been from old, from everlasting.
- Psalm 50:2-7 Out of Zion (the church), God has shined. Our God shall come and shall not keep silence.
- Isaiah 35:3-6 Behold your God will come -- open blind eyes and deaf ears.
- Matthew 11:5 The ministry of Jesus-the blind sees, lame walk, lepers cleansed, etc.
- Malachi 3:1 I will send my messenger who will prepare the way before me.
- Isaiah 61:1-2 Spirit of the Lord God is on me and anointed me to preach good tidings to the poor.
- Isaiah 6:1-5 Isaiah saw the Lord, Jesus, high and lifted up.
- John 12:39-41 Jesus speaks of the vision Isaiah had of the Lord.

COMPARATIVE REFERENCES OF THE ALPHA AND OMEGA, AND THE FIRST AND THE LAST

- Isaiah 48:12 I am **He** --the First and the Last

- Isaiah 44:6-8 The Lord, the King, the Redeemer -- the first and last and beside me there is no God.

- Revelation 1:8, 11, 18 Jesus, the Alpha and Omega -- the First and the Last.

- Revelation 21:3-7 He that sat upon the throne (God) is the Alpha and Omega.

- Genesis 17:1 God, the Almighty God to Abraham.

- Revelation 4:8,11 He (Jesus) is the Almighty.

- Matthew 28:18 All power given to Jesus both in Heaven and earth (the all powerful).

OLD AND NEW TESTAMENT COMPARISONS OF ONE GOD

- Isaiah 43:10-12 Before me there was no God formed neither will there be after me.

- Hosea 13:4 There is no Savior apart from me.

- Isaiah 46: 9-10 I am God - there is none like me.

- John 8:24 Jesus said that 'except you believe I AM He, you will die in your sins.'

- Isaiah 48:11 My Glory will I not give to another.

- John 5:23 We should honor the Son even (after the same manner) as the Father.

- Isaiah 45:5, 21-23 I am God, unto me every knee shall bow, and every tongue shall swear.

- Philippians 2:10-11 At the Name of Jesus, every knee shall bow, every tongue confesses.

- Isaiah 7:14 A virgin shall conceive and bear a son, His name called **Emmanuel.**

- Matthew 1:21, 23 Jesus called Emmanuel -- God with us.
- Isaiah 9:6 Name of the Son called: "Everlasting Father, The Mighty God".
- 1 Timothy 3:16 God was manifest in the flesh.
- Isaiah 54:5 Israel's Redeemer is the God of the whole earth.
- Zechariah 13:9 Israel will recognize Jesus as 'The Lord is my God'.
- Zechariah 14:9 The Lord (Jesus) shall be king over all the earth, and His name one.
- Isaiah 10:21 The remnant of Israel to return to the Mighty God (Jesus).
- Isaiah 43:11; 45:21 There is no Savior or Redeemer besides God.

REFERENCES LINKING JESUS AND GOD AS ONE

- Deuteronomy 6:4-9 The Lord our God is one Lord.
- Acts 2:36 God has made that same Jesus both Lord and Christ.
- Deuteronomy 10:17 The Lord your God is Lord of lords.
- Jeremiah 10:10 The Lord is the true God and King.
- 1 John 5:20 Jesus is the true God and Eternal Life.
- Jude vs 25 Jesus is the only wise God our Savior.
- 1 Timothy 6:15 Jesus is King of kings and Lord of lords.
- Revelation 17:14 The Lamb is Lord of lords and King of kings.
- 1 Timothy 1:17 Jesus is the King Eternal-the only wise God.
- Zechariah 14:9 The Lord shall be King over all the earth and His name is one.
- Titus 2:13-14 Looking for God and our Savior who gave Himself for us.

- Hebrews 1:1-3 Jesus is the express image of His person (the invisible God).

- Colossians 1:15-17 Jesus the image of the invisible God.

- Colossians 1:19; 2:9 In Him (Jesus) dwells all the fullness of the Godhead bodily.

- James 2:19 The devils believe there is one God.

- John 4:24 God is a spirit and must be revealed.

- John 1:18 No one has seen God at any time, but the Son has revealed Him.

- 1 Corinthians 12:3 No man can call Jesus Lord except by the Holy Ghost.

- John 14:9-11 The Father (Spirit) is in the Son (flesh).

- John 10:10 I and my Father are one (not one in purpose but one in fact).

- John 3:13 Jesus came from Heaven, even the Son of man who is in Heaven.

- John 13:3 Jesus came from God and went to God (one position to another).

- John 8:23 Ye (man) are from beneath, I (Jesus) am from above.

- 1 Corinthians 15:45-47 The last Adam is the Lord from Heaven.

- John 20:28 Thomas exclaims, 'My Lord and my God'.

- Exodus 3:14 To Moses, God said that "I AM that I AM". His name is "I AM".

- John 8:56-58 Jesus said that "before Abraham was I AM".

- Revelation 22:16 Jesus is the root and offspring of David.

GOD, THE CREATOR

- Genesis 1:1 In the beginning God created the Heaven and the earth.

- Genesis 2:7 God formed man from the dust of the earth.
- Job 33:4 The Spirit of God made me.
- Psalm 33:6 By the word of the Lord were the heavens made.
- Psalm 104:1 God's works of creation.
- Isaiah 40:28 The everlasting God, the Lord, the Creator of the ends of the earth.
- Isaiah 42:5 The Lord God created the heavens and gives breath to the people.
- Isaiah 44:24 The Lord maketh all thing-- alone (He needs no assistance).
- Isaiah 45:18 The Lord Himself formed the earth -- it was to be inhabited.
- Jeremiah 10:2 God made the world by His power.
- Malachi 2:10 One father has made us all.

JESUS, THE SON OF GOD AS CREATOR

- John 1:3, 10 The worlds were made by Him (the Word).
- Colossians 1:15-17 All things were created by Him and for Him.
- 1 Corinthians 8:6 Jesus, by whom are all things.
- Ephesians 3:9 Everything created by Christ Jesus.
- Hebrews 1:10 Thou Lord, in the beginning, hath laid the foundations of the earth.
- Revelation 4:8-11 Thou created all things.
- Revelation 10:6 Swear by Him (Jesus) who created Heaven and the things that are therein.
- Revelation 14:7 Worship Him that has made the heavens.

These are but a few of the hundreds of scriptural references in the Old and New Testaments that prove beyond any doubt the deity of Jesus and provide much details about who Jesus is. It is left for the reader to study these scriputral references and discover the hidden revelations. When one studies these biblical references with the intention to develop a meaningful relationship with God then you will come to know the most wonderful, magnificent, and awesome God who loved man so much that He came down from His glorious habitation to become one with man and to redeem his soul from eternal damnation. *"What is man, that thou shouldest magnify him? And that thou shouldest set thine heart upon him?"* (Job 7:17).

~11~
Jesus: the Only True God

There is much confusion within the ranks of Christians concerning the role of Jesus in the Godhead. Many acknowledge that Jesus Christ is a god and will agree with the notion that there is one God. However, to say that Jesus is that one true God, the majority of Christians are not willing to concede. It appears those who confess that there is one God, in most instances, do not know what it means, and they lack the spiritual knowledge and understanding to expound on what they confess to believe. The Godhead is a mystery and human understanding is insufficient to comprehend the secrecies of God because they are revealed to us by His Spirit (1 Corinthians 2:14; Matthew 11:25-26).

The concept of Trinity or God in three persons (Father, Son, and Holy Ghost) has become an embedded tradition in nearly every Christian doctrine. Its inception dates back around the third century after the day of Pentecost. History informs us the Council of Nicaea essentially introduced the Nicene Creed in 325 A.D. However, the Council of Constantinople made inroads for "the doctrine which the Council of Nicaea had left imperfect of three persons in one God" (Bellitto, 2002).

We, the three Emperors, will that our subjects follow the religion taught by St. Peter to the Romans, professed by those saintly prelates, Damascus, Pontiff of Rome, and Peter, Bishop of Alexandria, that they believe the one divinity of the Father, Son, and Holy Spirit, of majesty co-equal in the

Holy Trinity. We will that those who embrace this creed be called Catholic Christians. We brand all the senseless followers of other religions by the infamous name of heretics and forbid their conventicles to assume the name of Churches. The decree was endorsed and solidified in the names of Gratian, Valentinian II, and Theodosius. This was the birth of the doctrine of Trinity; as said by Dean Milman in his writing of the History of Christianity, 'the religion of the whole Roman world was enacted by two feeble boys and a rude Spanish soldier' (Schaff, 1882). Since that time, the overwhelming majority of men's eyes have been darkened and they have not been able to come to the truth (Stannus, 1883).

On one hand, the Trinitarians declare that we know there is one God and on the other hand they will divide the one God into two or three parts. It appears there is a lack of understanding due to the shortage of revelations through the Holy Ghost. It is through the illumination of the mind by the Holy Spirit that we understand the mysteries of God. God is not divided into many parts or personalities, but as one God assuming different manifestations all relative to each other for the purpose of redeeming and revealing Himself to man. God did not intend to confuse man nor are there scriptural references about the multiplicity of gods. He endeavored to instill in man through His first chosen people-Israel that He is one, and forewarned them lest the people were left to themselves to make images of Him in any form. "Hear, O Israel the Lord our God is One Lord" (Deuteronomy 6:4), and again "Unto thee it was shewed, that thou mightest know that the Lord he is God; there is none else beside him" (Deuteronomy 4:35). The theme throughout the Old Testament is, God is one and this one God would come in the fullness of time as a redeemer or savior to which the New Testament testifies.

God was invisible to the children of Israel; although, He occasionally appeared in a theophany or in the form of an angel unto them. When Jesus was born and came into the world, the invisible God that Israel knew by the name Jehovah was made visible in the form of the man Jesus Christ. The angel said that the child to be born was to be called Jesus. The prophet declared that this same child was to be called Immanuel, *"which being interpreted is, God with us"* (Matthew 1:21-23; Isaiah 7:14). Since God had emphatically declared that there is only one God, no other God before Him and none formed after Him (Isaiah 43:10-12; 44:6; 45:5-6, 9-10, 21-23), and that He (the eternal, invisible spirit) was that God then this child Jesus, which by the interpretation of His name is God with us, must be the same God abiding in a bodily form. In other words, Jesus is the invisible God made visible by a fleshly body in a way that we can see and understand (John 1:1, 14, 18). God as the eternal spirit could not be seen because no man has seen God in His essence at any time, but when the same spirit clothed itself with a fleshly body (a prepared house), the operations of the spirit expressed itself in terms that could be seen and understood by man (Hebrews 1:2-3; 10:5). This body was called the Son and had a beginning. It came into existence at the command of the Father (eternal, invisible spirit) through the womb of Mary. It had for its purpose the manifestation of God, a garment to cloth the invisible spirit the way God prepared Himself to taste our infirmities and temptations in order to succor us and to make this same body a lamb or sacrifice in the redemptive portion of His plan.

You may say then that there is a Father and a Son. Yes, there is a Father and a Son, but one combined together in one package, the visible revealing the invisible (Colossians 1:15-17), and not in a separated sense as human wisdom teaches two persons, an old man followed by a little boy. As stated before, God's manifestations or offices are all relative to each other. The relative position of the father to the son is that a father begets or causes a child to be conceived, which is eventually brought to birth by the mother. God as a spirit had no body but caused one to come into existence by commanding the fleshly seed within Mary's body to spring to life and come forth as a man child. The fleshly body became the Son of God because it was through the overshadowing of the Holy Ghost (Father) that it came into existence. To God, it was His house to dwell in. This does not mean there is a 'Father God' and a 'Son God', but it shows the relative position of the house to its begetter and dweller.

When one acknowledges Jesus as the only true God it is **not** a denial of the Father but to the contrary by acknowledging Jesus as the only true God is to possess the Father. *"Whosoever denieth the Son, the same hath not the Father; he that acknowledges the Son hath the Father also"* (1 John 2:23). Many individuals allow the flesh of Jesus to hide their eyes from His true identity. In the Old Testament, Israel could not behold the glory of God on the face of Moses, thus causing him to put a veil over his face as the body of Jesus a veil before men's eyes today, blocking the glory of God from their vision (1 Corinthians 3:13-16; John 10:33; Hebrews 10:20; Exodus 34:29-35). They cannot see God beholding the body because of their unbelief. People fail to acknowledge the Son in truth. If we confine Jesus to a human position alone or ascribe Him human and divine traits meanwhile separating Him from the Father then we have not appropriately acknowledged Him. But, if we say as Paul writes, *"For it pleased the Father that in him should all fullness dwell"* and again *"For in him dwelleth all the fullness of the Godhead bodily"* (Colossians 1:19; 2:9), then have we acknowledged the Son in His true setting.

All that God is, all the attributes of His spirit (wisdom, righteousness, creativeness counsel, understanding, might, knowledge, power, authority, and etc.) dwell directly, fully, and perfectly in the body of Jesus (Isaiah 11:2-3; Matthew 28:18). When one can see the Son and at the same time look beyond the veil (the body of flesh) and behold the manifestation of the invisible, eternal spirit (Father) then according to the Scripture they have the Father also. Human spirit or understanding does not reveal Jesus in this manner, but as it is written *"no man can say that Jesus is the Lord, but by the Holy Ghost"* (1 Corinthians 12:3) and again *"not the words which man's wisdom teacheth, but which the Holy Ghost teacheth; comparing spiritual things with spiritual"* (1 Corinthians 2:13).

Jesus was asked by Philip, *"Lord shew us the Father, and it sufficeth us."* Jesus, not willing that they be confused and scattered abroad looking for one other than Himself, He chided them by answering, *"Have I been so long time with you, and yet hast thou not known me, Philip, he that has seen me has seen the Father."* Notice, Jesus did not call Himself the Father, but simply told them where to look to see the Father, at Him. *"Believest thou not that I am in the Father, and the father in me? The words that I speak unto you I speak not of myself; But the Father that dwelleth in me, he doeth the works"* (John 14:7-10). This answer is the key that unlocks the mystery of the Godhead to understand what Jesus said, we will be able to see the Father and Son in their proper setting - **one in Jesus**. Therefore, to see the Father I must observe the Son and to obtain the Son is to obtain the Father. The Father and the Son are one in the same but different manifestations to accomplish interrelated purposes. To have one is to have both! If we have the Son, then we are partakers of the Spirit of Christ (Holy Ghost) which is the Spirit of God because there is one spirit (Ephesians 4:4-6; 1 Corinthians 12:13; Romans 8:9). When we have His spirit, we abide in His doctrine (2 John 1:9).

Naturally, a lively human body has a spirit which is invisible to the eyes, but its functions can be seen and understood as it manifests itself through the body. To see the body is the only way to see the spirit. As is with Jesus, the body was made to house the Eternal Spirit and we see the manifestation of the spirit in the face of Jesus Christ.

*"But ye are not in the flesh, but in the Spirit, if so be that the Spirit of God dwell **in** you. Now if any man have not the Spirit of Christ, he is **none of his"*** (Romans 8:9). Two things are evident in this verse. First, the Spirit of God and the Spirit of Christ are **one and the same spirit**. Since there is only one spirit (Ephesians 4:4-6), then Jesus must be God, and God (Spirit) must be in Jesus. See John 14:1-20. To see Jesus is to see the Father, *"**for the Father dwelleth in me"*** (vs. 9-10).

Furthermore, simply put without the Spirit of Christ (the Holy Ghost) one has no claim to Christ nor does Christ have claim to them.

Paul speaking of Jesus, calls Him *"the only wise God"* (1 Timothy 1:17), and again *"the only potentate, the King of kings, and Lord of lords" (1 Timothy 6:15)*. John identifies this same Jesus by saying: *"This is the true God, and eternal life"* (1 John 5:20), and lastly, Jude points to Jesus by declaring, *"to the only wise God our Saviour" (Jude 1:25)*. I have endeavored to show in a simple manner the only true God who has revealed Himself to us so that we who were without knowledge might know Him that is true, even Jesus.

~12~
Eternal Security
Vs.
Unconditional Eternal Security

The Doctrine of Unconditional Eternal Security has been around from the time of John Calvin, who received the credit for propagating this erroneous doctrine (Steele and Thomas, 1963). The fact that we can be eternally saved in Christ is not the issue, but to espouse the teaching that "once in Christ and never out" is a doctrine that is not supported by the apostles. *"Now unto him that is able to keep you from falling, and to present you faultless before the presence of his glory with exceeding joy, to the only wise God our Savior" (Jude 1:24-25).* See 2 Timothy 1:12 as well. We are assured by these and other references that God's power through the Holy Ghost is sufficient to sustain the saints in every situation and there is no justification to fail, at least not on God's part. There is no temptation greater than God's power.

The false hope promised by the creed of Unconditional Eternal Security is that if one regresses by returning to sinful practices and turns away from the faith, then they will be saved in the end, provided they were "once saved". This premise is totally in inaccurate because the Scripture declares, *"The soul that sinneth it shall die" (Ezekiel 18:4)* and *"When a righteous man turneth away from his righteousness, and committeth iniquity, and dieth in them; for his iniquity that he hath done shall he die" (Ezekiel 18:26).* Everyone of us has a part in maintaining our "saved status" but if we fail to do so, then there is the dreadful day of judgment to be faced. It is only as we obey and continue in the truth can our salvation be secured. Our responsibility is, *"if you love me, keep my commandments" (John 14:15).* "For as many as are led by the Spirit of God, they are the Sons of God" (Romans 8:14). *"If you continue in my word, then you are my disciples indeed" (John 8:31).* The keywords in each of the above references are, **keep, led, and continue**. To fail in these is to fail our responsibility of maintaining our own salvation. We will be presented *"holy and unblameable and unreprovable in his sight; if we continue in the faith grounded and settled and not moved away from the hope of the gospel" (Colossians 1:22-23).*

All of the promises God has made to His people are conditional. The promises made to Israel were on the condition they would keep His commandments and do His statutes (Deuteronomy 28). When they failed, God forsook them. When we fail the conditions set before us, He will leave us as well. However, if one sins, there is a process that God has provided for one to be restored to Him. The message is always to repent and turn towards Him, and confess and forsake the evil practices. If these conditions are met, He will receive us again. He takes no pleasure in the death of the wicked but pleads for man to repent and turn from evil that they might live (Ezekiel 18:30-32; Proverbs 28:13). God's purpose in extending mercy and grace to believers is to deliver them from sin so they might live the life of holiness and godliness (Ephesians 1:4; Colossians 1:21-23; Hebrews 12:14; 1 John 2:6). God did not deliver His people from sin to have them continue therein. Paul sets the record straight: *"Shall we continue in sin, that grace may abound? God forbid. How shall we, that are dead to sin, live any longer therein?" (Romans 6:1-2).* This should establish the fact that God's purpose is for us to live a sinless life in Christ.

The word 'if' is so important in the conditions God established for us to obey. Our security is assured in this

Scripture, "If you do these things, you will never fall" (2 Peter 1:10).

Unconditional Eternal Security declares in principle that if God received a person as His child by filling the individual with His spirit, then no matter what the person does they will be saved and not be eternally lost. Let us consider the following scriptural references and see the operations of God toward the sinning and disobedient individual.

> *Every branch in me that beareth not fruit he taketh away -- if a man abideth not in me, he is cast forth as a branch, and is withered; and men gather them, and cast them into the fire, and they are burned (John 15:2-6).*

In the epistle of Paul to the Roman church, he addressed Israel as a nation, discussed their failure to uphold the Word of God and became the cut off branches of the olive tree. He likens the Gentiles in the church to grafted branches from a wild olive tree, but God forewarns that if the natural branches were cut off and were not spared, then the grafted branches are subjected to the same treatment if they fail to continue in the faith (Romans 11:16-24).

We are warned in the church, *"Looking diligently, lest any man fail of the grace of God; lest any root of bitterness springing up trouble you, and thereby many be defiled"* (Hebrews 12:14-17). It is possible to "depart" from the living God. One cannot depart without first being in Christ as one cannot leave a room if they were not first in the room. *"Take heed, brethren, lest there be in any of you an evil heart of unbelief,"* in departing from the living God. We are made partakers of Christ if we hold the beginning of our confidence steadfast unto the end (Hebrews 3:12-14).

The nation of Israel could not enter into the promised land because of their unbelief, likewise, the saints are admonished about not entering into the promise God left the church if we suffer through unbelief and come short of entering into our rest (Hebrews 3:18-4:1). Moreover, *"God destroyed them [Israel in the wilderness] that believed not"* and this same thing will happen to the saints if we do not continue to believe the faith once delivered unto us (Jude 1:3-5). To be entangled again with the deadness of the Levitical Law called "the yoke of bondage" is to fall from grace, losing the hope of the gospel. Likewise, to return to the practice of sin and bondage is to fall from grace (Galatians 5:1-4). To have known righteousness and return to the bondage of sin is worse than never to have known what is right in the first place. These individuals will be judged by a higher law than those who are ignorant of God's way.

If after they have escaped the pollution of the world through the knowledge of the Lord and Savior Jesus Christ, and they are again entangled therein, and overcome, the latter end is worse with them than the beginning. For it had been better for them not to have known the way of righteousness, than after they have known it, to turn from the holy commandment delivered unto them (2 Peter 2:20-22).

God will not "blot out" the names of those who are overcomers, but the reverse is true if one **does not** overcome sin and this world, their names will be blotted out. To have one's name blot out, then it is safe to say the name was recorded once upon a time (Revelation 3:5; Revelation 21:7-8).

To sin willfully after receiving the knowledge of the truth, there is no more sacrifice for sin but a fearful looking for judgment (Hebrews 10:26-29). It is impossible to be once enlightened and taste the Holy Ghost and the powers of the world to come, then fall away to renew them again unto repentance seeing they have crucified the Lord afresh (Hebrews 6:4-8). However, let me say again, if one has committed a trespass there is a restorative and recovery plan provided by God's mercy: repentance, confession, and forsake the sin. But if the redemptive plan is ignored and one persists in living presumptuously in error, then there can be no recovery. Eternal damnation is the end for all who resist God's mercy and love (James 5:19-20). To convert (cause to return) a brother who errs from the truth is to save him from death and hide a multitude of sins.

Scripture states that there is a sin not unto death and a brother or sister can be restored through the pastoral ministry (1 John 5:16-17). There is also a sin unto death and such sin is not to be prayed for; there is no recovery available and it involves the presumptuous attitude and persistence in this sin. It is not a specific sin that is involved, but the attitude of commission (Jeremiah 7:16; 11:14; 14:11-12; Deuteronomy 21:22).

The Book of Romans (1:21-2:3) addresses the issue of Christian failure by saying if one fails to retain the knowledge of God in their mind and heart, they will become vain in their imaginations and God will give them up to uncleanness, vile affections, and a reprobate mind. Those who know right but continue to do wrong will not escape the judgment of God.

SCRIPTURAL REFERENCES

- Isaiah 59:2 Your sins have caused Him to hid His face from you.
- 1 John 1:6-7 To walk in darkness is to be out of fellowship with God.
- James 1:14-15 To be tempted and drawn away with one's own lust brings sin and death.
- Matthew 18:24-35 If we fail to forgive our brother, our forgiveness from God is revoked.
- Numbers 14:18 God will in no wise clear the guilty.
- 2 Thessalonians 1:8 and Romans 1:18 The wrath of God is against all ungodliness.
- 2 John 1:8 Look to yourselves that you lose not your reward.

If one is practicing those things the Bible describes as sin, then the individual will not enter the Kingdom of God. If one is filled with the Holy Ghost and lives a sinless lifestyle, then their obligation is to forsake the practices of their former life.

But if they return to the sins of the past then the wrath of God awaits them unless they repent and turn to do right.

> *Know ye not that the unrighteous shall not inherit the Kingdom of God? Be not deceived: neither fornicators, nor idolaters, nor adulterers, nor effeminate, nor abusers of themselves with mankind, nor thieves, nor covetous, nor drunkards, nor revilers, nor extortioners, shall inherit the Kingdom of God (1 Corinthians 6:9-10).*

The above scriptural reference applies to those who are filled with the Holy Ghost and still continue their sinful practices. The judgment is against the sin and whosoever is guilty will be judged by God.

The Book of Galatians (5:19-21) lists seventeen works of the flesh that disqualify one from the Kingdom of God: *"Adultery, fornication, uncleanness, lasciviousness, idolatry, witchcraft, hatred, variance, emulations, wrath, strife, seditions, heresies, envyings, murders, drunkenness, revellings and such like, shall not enter the Kingdom of God."* There are numerous scriptural references that provide a list of sins that will keep one from entering the Kingdom of God but these are just a few: (Revelation 21:8; Romans 8:12-13; Ephesians 5:3-7).

Scriptural references that illustrate the conditions which will bring eternal damnation although, an individual may have "once been saved":

- 2 Corinthians 13:5 Examine yourselves, know that Christ is in you that you be not reprobates.

- Titus 1:10-11 Vain and unruly talkers (teachers) that subvert whole houses.

- 2 Thessalonians 2:9-12 Those who will not believe the truth will receive a strong delusion from God that they may believe a lie.

- 2 Peters 2:1-2 False teachers will be among the church, teaching perverse things and deceive many who will be lost.

- 1 Corinthians 3:16-17 Those who defile the temple of God (my body) will God destroy.

- 1 Corinthians 9:27 Keep under the body, bring it into subjection (subdue its desires) that you do not become a castaway.

- 2 Peter 3:17 Beware lest ye also, being led away with the error of the wicked, fall from your own steadfastness.

- Galatians 2:18 If we build again those things which were once destroyed, we become transgressors.

- 2 Corinthians 12:21 Paul bewails many *"which have sinned already, and have not repented of the uncleanness, fornication and lasciviousness which they have committed."* By this, he implies that they are lost if they do not repent.

- 1 Timothy 4:1 *"The Spirit speaketh expressly, that in the latter times (present times), some shall depart from the faith giving heed to seducing spirits and doctrines of devils."* For one to depart from the faith, again they must have at one time been in the faith.

- 2 Peter 1:10 *"Wherefore the rather, brethren, give diligence to make your calling and election sure, for if ye do these things, ye will never fall."* If there was no danger of falling, why be so careful because in the end things will work out. Therefore, to show that there is a danger to fall, then be careful, diligent and watchful to preserve your soul in safety.

- 1 Thessalonians 3:3-5 There is a possibility of Satan tempting one and the labor of the gospel will be in vain for that soul.

To walk with God requires both faith in God and his Word. We do not walk by sight or the things of reason that presently appears. To be saved requires hearing the gospel and then reacting in obedience to that Word of Truth (Romans 6:17). This requires faith to step out on God's promise of deliverance and to receive the Holy Ghost. It takes faith to walk with God, even though circumstances seem against us. Our faith is in the power of God to help and deliver from the temptations, trials and adversities of the moment. There is no truth in the saying that "every man must sin a little". My faith is in the preserving power of God which enables me to escape the pitfalls of sin. Faith is required every day we walk with God because without it we cannot please Him (Hebrews 11:1-6). When we are willing to surrender our will to His will and be led by His spirit, then the adversary the devil will be unable to penetrate the defenses God provides for our safety. Paul declares,

> *I am crucified with Christ: nevertheless I live; yet not I, but Christ liveth in me: and the life which I now live in the flesh I live by the faith of the son of God, who loved me, and gave his life for me (Galatians 2:20).*

Apostle Peter reminds all Christians that through God's *"abundant mercy we were begotten unto a lively hope -- with an inheritance reserved in heaven for us--; that we are kept by the power of God through Faith unto salvation -- finally receiving the end of our faith, the salvation of the soul"* (1 Peter 1:3-9). When we, who have been reconciled through the blood of Christ are presented *"Holy, unblameable and unreprovable in his sight"* on the condition, *"if we continue in the faith" (Colossians 1:21-23).*

WARNING SIGNS

- Hebrews 12:15-17 Looking diligently lest any man fall from the grace of God.

- Hebrews 6:6-10 If one falls out of the grace of God, then it is impossible to renew them unto repentance.

- Hebrews 4:11 Let us labor to enter into that rest (eternal life) lest any man fall after the same example of unbelief (the unbelief of Israel in the wilderness).

- 1 Corinthians 10:12 Do not be over confident, "let him that thinketh he stands take heed lest he fall".

- 1 Corinthians 9:24-27 Discipline your body and its desires. Paul says, I bring under my body and bring it into subjection lest I become a castaway.

- Revelation 2:4-5 The church at Ephesus left their first love. Remember from whence you are fallen and repent or else your candlestick will be removed from its place.

- Revelation 3:14-22 The church at Laodicea, the current church age, is admonished that it is lukewarm and it will be "spewed out" of God's mouth. The condition is one of affluence, riches, and increased with goods and in need of nothing. But the church is unaware of its status with God as wretched, poor, miserable, blind, and naked. This age must overcome its faults before it can enter into His Kingdom.

The danger of falling away and how do we protect ourselves? Our trust and confidence in God coupled with the Holy Ghost is our only assurance of being securely saved. There must be a strong desire to be saved and to stay saved on our part before we can overcome the attempts by our enemy to seduce us into sin. Pleasing God and not ourselves must be the first priority of our life in Christ. Of the Seven church ages found in Revelation 2 and 3, only those who overcame the conditions of their time were able to stand in God's presence and enjoy the pleasures of His Kingdom. Our attitude towards sin is very important, if we do not regard all sin as total repugnant before God, then we will become careless and indifferent to our responsibilities before God. The love of God's Word and its place in our heart is another critical deterrent against sin (Psalm 119:9-11). Attributes of an overcoming child of God includes faith, desire, determination, perseverance, vision, resistance, and separation from evil.

NOTE THE FOLLOWING BIBLICAL REFERENCES

- 1 Peter 1:3-5 We are kept by the power of faith ready to be revealed.

- 2 Timothy 1:12 I am persuaded God is able to keep that which has been committed unto Himself until that day.

- Philippians 2:12-13 Work out your own salvation with fear and trembling. Because it is God which worketh in you both to will and to do of His good pleasure.

- Ephesians 3:20 He is able to do exceeding, abundantly above all we may ask or think.

- Jude 1:24-25 He is able to keep you from falling and to present you faultless in that day.

- Hebrews 7:25 He is able to save to the uttermost those who come to Him.

The doctrine of predestination is a central part of Unconditional Eternal Security and is associated with the sovereignty of God. Essentially, the ideology imposes on its followers that God predetermines before an individual is born whether he or she will be saved. If one is predestined by God's sovereignty to go astray, eternally damned, then there is no way to redeem the individual. On the contrary, if one is predestined to be saved by God's choice, then there is no way they can be eternally damned. The doctrine describes that people have no control or choice over their eternal destiny and God will save them at the very end even though they may sin to their last breath. This premise is false and the scriptural references are ample evidence of the error in this ideology.

There are only two predestined entities in the Bible, entities determined to be and no possibility of change. Persons are not predestined with the exception of Jesus Christ, the Son of God. His coming was predetermined in God's plan of salvation before the foundation of the world and could not be altered from God's original purpose. We are redeemed by *"the precious blood of Christ as of a lamb without blemish and without spot, who was foreordained before the foundation of the world"* and *"whose names are not written in the Book of Life of the lamb slain from the foundation of the world"* (1 Peter 1:19-20; Revelation 13:8). The second is the church, *"According as he has chosen us (the church) in him before the foundation of the world, that we should be Holy and without blame before him in love"* (Ephesians 1:4). The church also known as the body of Christ is predestined to Heaven and not the individuals who make up the church.

One of the best examples that I have heard about predestination: a plane that is scheduled to fly from New York at 10 AM will arrive in South Africa 17 hours later. As a ticket holder, if I missed the opportunity to board that flight, the plane will arrive at its predetermined destination. The plane was predestinated for South Africa regardless of if I missed my flight or I was onboard. As a Christian, if I am not in good standing with God then I will miss the opportunity to be part of His plan and will not arrive at the predetermined destination of the church. God knows who will be saved and who will not because of His foreknowledge. He is the omniscient God. However, this foreknowledge does not compel an individual to believe nor does it cause hindrance in one's faith. Faith in the Word of God is left to the individual's choice (Luke 10:20). God's foreknowledge offers Him access to foresee the beginning and end of matters before they happen and is privy to our thoughts "afar off" (Psalm 139:1-4). *"The Lord is a God of knowledge, and by him actions (motives) are weighed"* (1 Samuel 2:3).

God uses individuals to fulfill His will because of His knowledge of their character. For instance, Pharaoh's heart was hardened because God knew his heart would not change even with severe chastisement and judgments. God did not make Pharaoh a vessel of dishonor, but knowing his nature, used him as a vessel to fulfill His purpose. God told Moses, I know what Pharaoh will do and he became a convenient tool in God's hands to carry out the punishment of Egypt (Exodus 3:19-20). Pharaoh was not forced to act as he did, but God's foreknowledge predicted what Pharaoh would do. In the beginning Pharaoh hardened his own heart, after which God hardened it knowing he would not change (Exodus 8:15, 19, 32; 9:7, 12, 34; 10:1, 20). Another example: Cyrus, King of Persia, and King Josiah were both prophesied by name before they were born to fulfill certain activities in their lifetime (Isaiah 44:28; 2 Chronicles 36:22; Ezra 1:1-4; 1 Kings 13:2; 2 Kings 23:16). Jeremiah was called while yet in his mother's womb (Jeremiah 1:5), but it was his choice to obey God's directives (v. 17).

If we have no choice in our eternal destiny, then why do we preach the gospel and why hear God's Word to make a choice towards or against salvation? *"I have set before thee this day life and good, and death and evil - therefore choose life that both thou and thy seed might live"* (Deuteronomy 30:15-20). Elijah challenged Israel: *"How long halt between two opinions? If the Lord be God, follow him; but if Baal, then follow him"* (1 Kings 18:21). The New Testament is full of invitations to respond to the gospel.

> *Come unto me all ye that labor and are heavy laden, and I will give you rest"* (Matthew 11:28); "Go into the world and preach the gospel to every creature. He that believeth and is baptized shall be saved; but he that believeth not shall be damned" (Mark 16:15; Colossians 1:23). "For God so loved the world that he gave his only begotten son, that whosoever believeth in him should not perish, but have eternal life"* (John 3:16).

These are a few biblical references that give us the opportunity to choose and determine the way we want to go. Choosing life or death is our responsibility and God does not make that choice for us. He gives us the information that will enable us to make a wise choice. God bless you as you read.

Author

Dr. Harry L. Herman was born on November 14, 1924 in Indianapolis, Indiana. He was baptized in Jesus name and filled with the Holy Ghost on July 5, 1949 and grew up in the church-Christ Temple, Indianapolis. He served in the U.S. Army in the Pacific Theatre in World War II.

On October 9, 1949, he married Jenny Rea "Jerry" Herman, and the Lord blessed them with five sons. Dr. Herman and his wife were active members of Christ Temple. He served in almost every department of the church including served as Assistant Pastor before being called to pastor Christ Temple in Detroit in 1965. He received his Certificate of Fellowship for the ministry in March 1955 with the A.B.S.A. He became the chairman of the Sunday School Department and the assistant chairman of the Young People's Department in the A.B.S.A.

He was elevated to the office of bishop in the Pentecostal Assemblies of the World, Inc. in March 1989 and consecrated in August 1989. He has served on many committees: the Pulpit Committee, License and Credential Committee, Chairman of the Judicial Committee, and Director of the I.C.E.A. He is a well-known Bible teacher who stands firmly on the Oneness doctrine. He received his early teaching from his parents, who received their teaching from the late Bishop G. T. Haywood, and Elder Robert F. Tobin. His ministry was further enhanced by reading Bishop Haywood's writings and sitting under the late Bishop Morris E. Golder, and the late Bishop Willie Lee. He served as Diocesan Bishop of the Minnesota, Wisconsin, and Dakotas Council for nearly seven years before being appointed Diocesan Bishop of the Northern District Council (Michigan) from 1996-2013. He was elected Chairman of the Council in 1984 for two terms and served as District Elder for 11 years.

He moved his family to Kalamazoo at the invitation of the late Bishop Ross P. Paddock in September 1970 to become the Assistant Pastor of Christ Temple in Kalamazoo. Bishop Paddock resigned June 5, 1972 as Pastor and Bishop Herman was elected as the Pastor where he faithfully served until January 31, 2010. He has a perfect record in Sunday School for 34 years as a teacher. He received an honorary Doctor of Divinity from Aenon Bible College in 1994, and earned a Doctor of Theology and a Doctor of Divinity from the International Apostolic College in 1995. He is an esteemed counselor and teacher of young ministers, pastors, and married couples.

Afterword

The Fundamentals of Pentecostal Oneness content was applied in the church where the author pastored. The original church consisted of a small congregation and these fundamentals were instrumental in establishing the leadership of the church and directing the vision of the ministry. These fundamentals were written as a teaching tool for those new to the faith and aspiring ministers who needed to understand the fundamentals of the precious Oneness message, we cherish. It is important to know the truth before one can teach it.

Notes

Bellitto, C. (2002). *The General Councils: A History of the Twenty-One General Councils from Nicaea to Vatican II.* Mahwah, NJ: Paulist Press.

Box, N. (1996). *A Concise History of the Early Church.* New York, NY: Continuum International Publishing Group.

Chaswick, H. (1993). *The Early Church.* New York, NY: Penguin.

Dimock, N. (1911). *History of the Church.* London, UK: Longmans, Green & Company.

Durant, W. (1950). *The Story of Civilization: The Age of Faith, 4.* New York, NY: Simon and Schuster.

Erikson, E. H., & Erikson, J. M. (1998). *The Life Cycle Completed.* New York, NY: W. W. Norton & Company.

Forbush, W. B. (1978). *Fox's Book of Martyrs.* Grand Rapids, MI: Zondervan.

Hanson, R. P. C. (1985). *Studies in Christian Antiquity.* New York, NY: Bloomsbury T & Clark.

Haywood, G. T. (n.d.). *The Birth of the Spirit in the Days of the Apostles.* Indianapolis, IN: Christ Temple Bookstore.

Haywood, G. T. (n.d.). *The Resurrection of the Dead.* Indianapolis, IN: Christ Temple Bookstore.

Haywood, G. T. (n.d.). *The Victim of the Flaming Sword.*

Indianapolis, IN: Christ Temple Bookstore.

Jacobsen, D. G. (2006). *A Reader in Pentecostal Theology: Voices from the First Generation.* Bloomington, IN: Indiana University Press.

Lakin, C. (1990). *Dispensational Truth or God's Plan and Purpose in the Ages.* Glenside, PA: Rev Clarence Larkin Estate.

McBrien, R. P. (1995). God. *In The HarperCollins Encyclopedia of Catholicism. (pp. 564-576). New York, NY:* The HarperCollins Publishers, Inc.

McGiffert, A. C. (1954). *A History of Christian Thought.* New York, NY: Charles Scribner's Sons.

Paddock, R. P. (2004). *The Seven Stages of the First Resurrection.* Piqua, OH: Ohio Ministries, Inc.

Parchia, E. (n.d.). *The Doctrine of Unconditional Eternal Security Factor or Fallacy.*

Schaff, P. (1882). *History of the Christian Church.* New York, NY: Charles Scribner's Sons.

Stannus, H. (1883). *History of the Origin of the Doctrine of the Trinity in the Christian Church.* Oxford, UK: Bodleian Library.

Steele, D. N., & Thomas, C. C. (1963). *The Five Points of Calvinism: Defined, Defended, Documented.* Phillipsburg, NJ: Presbyterian & Reformed Publishing Co.

Thayer, J. (1996). *Greek-English Lexicon of the New Testament.* Peabody, MA: Hendrickson Publishers.

Tobin, R. (n.d.). *The Principles of the Doctrine of Christ.*

Vine, W. E., White, W., & Unger, M. F. (1984). *Vine's Complete Expository Dictionary: Of Old and New Testament Words (1st Ed.).* Nashville, TN: Thomas Nelson, Inc.

www.ingramcontent.com/pod-product-compliance
Lightning Source LLC
Chambersburg PA
CBHW071406160426
42813CB00084B/581